MAKE MONEY AS A FREELANCE WRITER

Your Simple Starter Guide To Setting A Freelance Writing Business And Earning Money From Home In As Little As 30 Days

JOHN ROBERTSON

Copyright © 2016 By John Robertson | All Rights Reserved.

Table Of Contents

The Importance of Building Your Freelance Copywriting Blueprint 1

Benefits of Freelance Writing Jobs 2

Achieveing a Flexible Lifestyles Through Freelance Copywriting 4

Whar Is a Freelance Writer? 7

What Is Copywriting? 10

How to Get Started With Copywriting 18

The Basics of Setting Up Your Copywriting Business 20

The Basic Mechanism of Copywriting 25

Do You Have What It Takes To be a Freelance Writer? 29

Becoming Invaluable By Making Your Client's Life Easier 36

Jumping Into Freelance Copywriting 38

Freelamce Writing : The Essentials 41

Home Business Set-Up 43

How To Get Lucrative Freelance Writing Jobs 49

Where to Look for Freelance Copywriting Jobs 53

Where You Can Find Freelance Writing Opportunities 55

Tips In Getting Freelance Writing 58

Marketing Your Services 61

Simple Methods Of Marketing Your Copywriting Business 64

Elements of Effective Sales Copy: The Sales Page 69

Bonus Chapter: Freelance Paralegal (Advanced)...................... 73

Conclusion 75

The Importance of Building Your Freelance Copywriting Blueprint

The home business market is teeming with entrepreneurs who want to pursue a better and more flexible working environment. Entrepreneurs are using their creative ideas to make a business for themselves.

Entrepreneurs are starting new businesses in record numbers. They are reviving stale ones and even embarking on joint ventures, pooling resources and finding success within hot niche markets where their skills and creativity are consistently in demand.

Many aspiring home-based entrepreneurs seek out methods of using their existing skill set and talents, to generate an income from the comforts and convenience of their home office.

Are you ready to join the ranks of those who have carved out a name for themselves and dramatically improved their lifestyles?

Let's get started!

JOHN ROBERTSON

BENEFITS OF FREELANCE WRITING JOBS

Doing extra work is the way to go in this day and age especially if you want to earn an extra amount of money. With the rising prices of food and other basic commodities, it is not surprising that the trend is becoming the rule now rather than an exception. And more and more people are actually looking for additional sources of income especially if you have many mouths to feed.

Most are now working for more hours than they should be, holding more than one job at a time. Some who have to render long hours of time in their regular work, use their day off or the weekends to do some extra work. Some work on the local cinema or mall for a few hours while others do some babysitting on the side after office hours.

One of the alternative for people who wish to make extra money is to do freelancing. Most say that freelancing is actually better than holding part time jobs. This is especially true with writers by profession who can actually make use of their talent and their expertise to earn extra pay.

Writers are very much in demand these days because of the rising demands for their services in websites. Writers are needed to do online content and to update websites in order to boost site visits and viewerships. The pay is oftentimes better and the hours are not so long. Some even do freelancing for full-time.

But before you decide to venture into the professional world of freelance writing, read on. Below are some of the advantages that freelance writing jobs have.

Flexible hours

Freelance writing do not have a prescribed schedule. You will not be asked to render a specific number of hours. This means that you own your time and you will determine the schedule that you will have for a specific time period. Often freelance writers will be given a specific time period in which they can finish the assignments. The shorter the time period given, the higher the pay. In fact, they can actually negotiate for the pay if the assignment is a rush one.

Because of the flexible hours, freelance writers can do several assignments in one day and accept more than one freelancing assignments at one time. This will mean higher income for them and of course no stress to do finish the job. This of course will depend on how you will manage your time.

Family matters

Freelancing is also a viable option for people who can have to take care of children or who need to do something for the family. This is especially true with women who need to be at home to take care of the children. Freelancing is a good option to earn money and still stay at home. After all, you can just write almost anywhere.

Training while earning

Compared to other part time jobs that you can do, doing freelance writing jobs will allow you to use what you are already doing. This will allow you to increase your knowledge and to widen your experience. Your part time work will also enable you to practice what you know and use your expertise. What is more, every freelance writing job that you do is a feather in your cap, which you can add up to your credentials.

JOHN ROBERTSON

ACHIEVEING A FLEXIBLE LIFESTYLES THROUGH FREELANCE COPYWRITING

Individuals who want to enjoy the work at home lifestyle look for creative and lucrative ways to be at home with their children, generate additional income or includes new entrepreneurs who are looking to create a sound, residual income.

For many, work at home ideas that are lucrative and flexible take precedence over ideas that may perhaps be easier to implement. Knowing this helps an aspiring entrepreneur to lean or not lean towards any idea in particular.

The business must also offer certain benefits to get their attention, or at least have a desirable end result to be seriously considered.

This is because in many cases, the entrepreneur has already tried a traditional working arrangement or work hours and is not satisfied. They may look to try something else. But what? And why?

Practical Home Business

People are seeking different things in a home business. However, the common denominator could be flexibility, convenience, ease of start-up, or profit potential. It all depends on the needs and wants of the home business entrepreneur.

For instance, while it may be easier to start a home business doing home parties, the time that it takes to set-up, deliver and process the event may become overwhelming.

These home parties can be inflexible and infringe n many schedules. This type of home business therefore may not be as flexible or convenient as another.

The goal of the home business owner is to find or start a business that is fairly easy to implement, yet able to generate a significant but fair income.

While there are many businesses that can certainly offer these benefits, there is a home business in particular that can offer you:

- Flexibility
- Convenience
- Lucrative income
- Passive income
- Potential for growth
- Repeat business

What kind of business offers you all of these characteristics?

A career in copywriting has the potential to offer you a flexible home business that is both convenient and lucrative. Copywriting is not new, and has been in existence for decades, if not centuries in terms of marketing concepts, ideas and brands.

The copywriting skill has evolved significantly over the years, however, but still remains a very core and sound business to get started in if you possess the creative talents necessary to be able to craft compelling sales copy that evokes emotional responses.

For anyone who is serious about starting their career in copywriting or in writing engaging, action-inducing copy has to but just look at copywriting as a sound but lucrative business to pursue.

WHAR IS A FREELANCE WRITER?

An online freelance writer is someone who writes articles, eBooks, web content, newsletters, ezine, and anything else. They are paid to write up interesting, educational articles that capture their audience. They are paid to fill content on the web. All the writing that a freelance writer does is usually the buyers copyright forever. It is a very fun career if you like to write because you are always learning about new things. The greatest part of it is the fact that you get to make your own hours and work from the comfort of your own home. It is great for stay at home mothers or handicapped people or people with very busy schedules. You write on your own time as long as you finish your projects on your due date. Depending on what you write, you could get paid about 500 dollars for an eBook, not bad.

A freelance writer finds their projects many different ways, such as word of mouth or referrals, or online services. Elance is an online service where employers can post jobs for freelancers, programmers, tech support, etc. There are many sites like this one where you can go to find work, although there is usually a monthly fee you must pay to get these desirable jobs. When accepting a job, if there is no provided contract, a freelance writer should always create an informal contract describing the project, due date, fees, etc.

The work that freelance writers submit should be fresh and creative. It should NEVER be plagiarized. A freelance writer will always spell check their work and make sure it sounds great. Having a portfolio of your work is an excellent idea because it shows how great of a writer you are under varied projects. Taking some online writing classes will also keep you learning new ways to write better. Details always count so make sure you keep up to date and always write from your heart.

Freelance jobs have attracted the masses due to their benefits such as being able to be their own boss, flexi time working schedules, spending valuable time with the family, and income can be unlimited.

Before taking up freelance jobs, the person has to decide if his business needs an Internet connection. The best known home based jobs are by selling home made products.

Once it is decided to go for an online job, he or she has to choose a freelance job, which compliments his experience, knowledge and expertise. Internet has created umpteen opportunities for freelance professionals in almost all the fields like web development, telemarketing, copywriting, proof reading etc.

Time management is very important in freelance jobs. The person needs to be very organized and focused to deliver the services and goods on the said time. Although doing a freelance job will facilitate spending a valuable time with the family, it should not hinder with the execution of the job.

The basic requirements of the freelance jobs are the resources and tools. They need to be in place like the high speed internet connection for downloading and uploading information etc. The person has to set a target to achieve the monthly income desired and work towards attaining it.

When working independently doing freelance jobs, there is a possibility to get diverted easily; as there is no manager or boss to monitor the actions and behavior. This calls for self discipline and finishing the job before the deadline to succeed as a freelance professional.

The work place for doing freelance jobs has to be quiet to do the work in a focused manner and free from distractions. Also, it should give a feeling of a work area than of a home atmosphere. Cluttering of materials should be avoided, as it has a tendency to irritate the person doing job.

When doing freelance jobs, the freelancer should be on a lookout for new projects constantly. Also accepting too many offers beyond the capability should be avoided. Projects which can be completed within the time frame should be selected to be got and delivered on time and then he can accept new projects. Work should be comfortably done rather than done in a stretched manner.

What Is Copywriting?

Copywriting is a very specialized form of writing that requires certain skills, primarily that you are able to engage a reader, cause them to think about specific situations and motivate them into taking action based on providing them with a solution to an existing problem.

Writing copy (copywriting) is a sophisticated form of communication with an express purpose, typically targeted at companies or individuals who can make buying decisions.

Copywriting is used to inform, sell, distribute, market and promote products or services that are designed purposefully to entice individuals or other businesses to buy.

Businesses know that consumers make buying decisions based on a mixture of facts and emotions and often, emotions dominate their decisions.

This is why the market is in such high demand because the average consumer will buy based on his emotions and copywriters focus on triggering those emotions AND controlling the outcome of how a reader responds to these feelings (purchases a product, subscribes to a newsletter, completes a survey, etc.(

There is a significant amount of attention placed on words, choice of words, word placement, tone (the voice of your copy) and once again, emotional call outs that appear within a copywriting piece.

Since all of these elements together are essential for success, it's no doubt that seasoned copywriters who have mastered the art of creative selling are in such demand, and in turn, are some of the highest paid writers in the industry.

The process of copywriting involves crafting compelling, inviting copy whose main goal is to entice readers to buy. In the end, that is the desired result.

Although not all of the readers will buy, the target market is only being satisfied by a small percentage of decision-makers.

In the process of copywriting, the writer will give ideas, facts and information that will better equip the reader (or listener) to make a decision based on their interpretation. It is the copywriters responsibility to first capture attention, engage the reader, provoke emotion and then funnel that emotion into prompting the reader into making a decision, or taking an action of some kind. The way that the material is presented and interpreted by the copywriter will ultimately be responsible for the success or failure of the sales pitch.

The challenge for the copywriter is to create a positive interpretation for the reader that is in favour of the product or service that is being offered without coming off strong (unless that is the intended voice of the message.(

For the most part, copywriters don't have to sell at all, instead, they present the option of success or failure to the reader and leave them little choice.

For example, on a salespage focused on making money online, a copywriter could highlight the reasons why the reader may have failed repeatedly when trying to start an online business.

They could assure them that it's not their fault, that they were misled and even deceived deliberately by other marketers.   Then, the copywriter could warn the reader that unless they take action and purchase a solid blueprint to success, that they are likely to continue losing time and money with unsuccessful strategies, only to find themselves in the same situation they are in now, a year later.

This evokes the emotion of both fear and failure. Fear, that they will be scammed, lied to, misled, deceived and of failing in terms of losing time and money by not purchasing the featured product.

Copywriting techniques are curtailed and customized to fit the challenge that the writer is drafting the copy for, and each project may call upon the copywriter to use a different style, voice or strategy.

For example, certain marketing agencies prefer that copywriters create advertisements that take a personal approach, where it speaks directly to the reader, empathizes with them, and gives the feeling that the writer has their best interest at heart, while other marketing companies prefer a direct, hard sale, where the copywriter takes a more aggressive approach to marketing and subsequently, selling the product.

Regardless of the style used, the copywriter should always be able to create a sense of urgency, so the reader feels compel to act quickly, or risk losing the opportunity that is being presented to them.

There are three emotions that are often evoked from effective copywriting:

1 - Urgency

Good copywriting will create a sense of urgency. It will make the reader feel like they need to react quickly, or to make a critical decision at that very moment.

Well-written copy will have the reader ready to respond even before they reach the end of the sales letter or copy that they're reading.

Copywriters will implement "emotional pulls" throughout the copy, to ensure that they are able to captivate readers who skim the sales page, and material.

What kinds of copy call upon a sense of urgency?

An example of this would be the sale of exercise products or weight-loss information. If the copy is well-crafted and cleverly written, the reader would be ready to place her order even before she reaches the end of the page, because not only are they given a clear picture of their current situation (before), they are also given a vivid image of what they can accomplish if they take action (after.(

Spend some time watching late night infomercials if you're interested in seeing some of the most well written, emotion driven advertising material available. Take notes of the terms, wording and phrases they use, and how they often weave in both fear and relief by first presenting the problem and offering a clear solution to those desperate for help.

Since infomercials are also some of the most expensive forms of marketing, the advertising tactics have been analyzed, tested and proven to work. It's simply one of the best ways to garner ideas for your own copy by seeing what works (as well as what pulls your own strings, and activates emotional triggers based on your personal lifestyle.(

2 - Fear

The type of fear that well-written copy evokes is the idea that without the service or product being advertised, that the reader will somehow experience a negative "side effect" (such as failing, continuing to experience pain, causing their situation to become worse, etc). The reader may feel that without it, they are incomplete, bound to fail or be left behind.

Perfect examples are advertisements focused on online businesses where competition is stiff and entrepreneurs are concerned about others gaining a foothold in their market.

Compelling sales copy would address these situations and explain how without the information readily available to them, they stand a chance of letting their competition take control of their markets, or worse, push them out of their existing niches.

The solution?

To purchase the product (course, training, newsletter, etc) and be part of an inner circle, ahead of the competition, gaining inside knowledge.

Essentially, if the reader feels that NOT having what is being sold in the copy is detrimental, he will be at a disadvantage.

Using the weight-loss industry as another example, the reader may experience fear if they do not quickly purchase the product that will help them shed pounds quickly that they will gain more weight, become more unhealthy and perhaps never be able to recover again.

3 - Anticipation And Excitement

Motivating a reader to look to the future and anticipate upcoming products or information is a very effective method used by copywriters online, especially those that are creating marketing material for recurring products (membership websites, newspapers, newsletters, etc (The copy will enlighten the reader, and paint a clear picture of what is currently available as well as what is being created, just for them.)

By focusing on showcasing their current situation and how it will improve with future material offered, copywriters have helped newspapers attain loyal subscribers, ezine marketers to build massive lists of active buyers, and websites to experience a flood of prospects interested in keeping a pulse on current developments and future launches.

Again, with the weight-loss example, well-crafted copy can invoke a feeling of anticipation and drive the reader towards a desired result. (10 Pounds in 10 Days!, and other similar headlines will cause the reader to envision their future, and how much their lives can change if they remain a member and digest the material as it becomes available every month, week, year.(

Another way that excitement is used within ad copy is in the backend funnel, where a copywriter continues to lead the buyer through the sales system where they are offered additional products and purchases while they are in an active buying state. Copywriting should never stop at the sales page but continue through every element of the process, through the ordering system, straight through to the final step.

Anticipation and excitement will make the reader do things that they may not otherwise consider. Work to incorporate this emotion into your copy and you've created a hook for your piece.

These three emotions vary in intensity and relativity from one reader to the next. Certain people will respond to these tactics differently, but it's the job of the copywriter to reach out the majority by using time tested, proven methods of evoking and controlling emotional responses.

What Copywriting Is NOT

With copywriting, words are everything and the placement of words is even more critical. It's important to say the right things at the right time to the right people.

However, it is not always easy to get that right or to find ways where this will work 100% of the time.

1 - Copywriting is not an exact science

Companies and people are so vastly different. A good copywriter has to customize his content to appeal to the reader and gain the desired result, however, what works for one group of people won't always work for another and so you'll need to research your target audience, analyze what has worked in the past, and craft your copy to integrate similar tactics. That's the goal.

But even with well-crafted copy, it's still not guaranteed to yield results, which is why even the best copywriters work to consistently tweak their copy, and improve results with in-depth testing.

2 - Copywriting is not the same as article writing

Article writing is simply the sharing and disseminating of information in a formatted fashion. Copywriting will entice the reader to buy.

Articles will share and impart information to the reader that doesn't lean towards a sale or decision. While articles can help to "pre-sell" readers, preparing them for the full sales page, article writing is typically a more passive method of communication, rather than a direct one.

3 - Copywriting Can Be Short Or Lengthy

Contrary to what you may have been taught, copywriting does not have to be lengthy to be effective.

Copywriting is best known in the form of long sales copy pages, brochures or newsletters, however the actual copy composition does not have to be lengthy to accomplish its goal as long as you ensure that you have incorporated the most important elements and have structured your sales pages to trigger the emotions you are aiming for.

Som the key point here is this: length does NOT equate to effectiveness.

JOHN ROBERTSON

HOW татай TO GET STARTED WITH COPYWRITING

First, let's take a look at what copywriting really is and how becoming a copywriter can possibly be the best choice for you as a home business entrepreneur.

The best way you can enter the writing business is to start with freelance copywriting. Freelance copywriting is a good money-yielding job. Every business activity requires marketing the materials in the written form, whether big or small. Freelance copywriting may involve materials right from tiny advertisements to big training manuals. Web marketing is very effective to run the business in a fast way. Web marketing involves web sales pages, online catalog copy, web site copy, pay per click advertising etc. Actually the opportunities for freelance copywriting are unlimited. There is no prerequisite condition to enter this field of copywriting. To earn good money through copywriting, the freelancer should get organized in the first place and should know how to write, so that a freelancer can get the maximum benefit out of this profession.

Almost all the businesses have their web pages and they need to keep their page rankings. Unless and until the web pages are refreshed with new contents, they cannot keep their page rankings high. Failing to keep the content refreshed might also result in a setback to the business as the ranking might drop. There are millions of such websites, which require the assistance of the freelance copywriters. Imagine the scope for copywriting profession for yourself. Freelance copywriting requires a bit of imagination and creativity to excel in the field. The first step is to find companies, which can pay the freelance copywriters adequately for writing their content. The topic should be understood properly, and then the information necessary for it needs to be collected. Organizing the facts and presenting it with originality is the secret of success of a freelance copywriter.

Copywriting portfolio of the freelance copywriter is very crucial in getting good assignments, as the copywriting portfolio will consist of the materials he has written like the brochures, direct mailer samples, advertisements, web sales pages etc. It is always good to get the consent of the client before adding the work to your portfolio, the one you wrote for them.

The legitimate way of building the portfolio of the freelance copywriter is to work for a local agency as an intern copywriter. Even though the money gained during such period is of less value, the experience gained will be of great value. Also the person will get good contacts, which can be useful while becoming a freelance copywriter.

JOHN ROBERTSON

The Basics of Setting Up Your Copywriting Business

A home business in copywriting can be started relatively quickly and easily, with a very low investment cost.

There are many entrepreneurs who enjoy the flexible lifestyle as a solid home business who have started their copywriting service simply by writing out samples and building an online portfolio that showcases their writing styles, their ability to adapt to different markets, and to take on different voices (and approaches) to target audiences.

As a sole proprietor of the business, you have the flexibility to sub-contract your writing work out or do it all yourself.

The necessary steps you need to take to become a copywriter are as follows:

1 - Decide on your genre

What kind of writing do you want to provide as a copywriter? Decide on what type of copywriting style you're interested in writing about, or if you are interested in multiple markets, make sure that you are able to take on different writing styles.

As a copywriter myself, it's not always easy to be able to write in different voices, where your message may read the same way but generate a different response based on the target market. Take some time to personally write about different topics, markets and products, using passive, aggressive, soft and hard selling copy, to determine what style you are best at, and what styles you prefer.

Will you specialize in newsletter writing, magazine feature writing or article writing?

If you know the type of writing that you will concentrate on, it will help you develop materials and resources targeted towards that market. To get a better idea of what type of writing genre to pursue, take a look at online and print ads to see what's popular, what methods are widely used and to what niche audiences the pitch is made.

After you decide on your writing genre, then develop a solid plan and course of action to administer your ideas, and begin to construct a website that highlights all of your services, price structure and samples.

If you have not yet secured a client or testimonials from past work, don't let this hinder you from taking action.

Begin writing in your free time, and consistently working towards expanding your knowledge, your writing vocabulary, and your experience by researching existing copywriters, dissecting effective copy, analyzing what works, and what doesn't, and then doing your best to restructure this in your own style.

2 - Assess your experience

What kind of experience do you have? How does that experience help you in your writing endeavours?

A writer's experience is only second to the passion that he possesses to effectively do a good job. Without experience as a writer, you may lack the necessary foundation to get started on this career path.

While you may not feel that you have enough experience to begin, if you dedicate yourself to learning and mastering this trade, it won't be long before you are able to attract new clients and new business.

Any kind of writing experience can help jump-start your writing career in copywriting. Whether that experience is in basic content writing, magazine writing or in a corporate setting, you can use the foundational tools to get started in copywriting.

Don't discount any previous writing work done, thinking that it isn't professional enough. Likewise, don't wait until you get what may be deemed "enough" experience.

Start with where you are and with what you've got to jump start your writing career.

3 - Set your goals

What goals do you want to achieve as a writer? Do you simply want to be known as a writer or do you want to work towards achieving tangible goals?

Writers should always start out with a tangible, reachable writing goal within their sights. The writing business is very intense and can become very discouraging for some.

Setting goals help to keep you on track and position you for success.

To help you stay on the track towards success, write down your goals and refer to them often, for follow-up and for inspiration. NEVER over-reach!

Instead, set goals that can be reached, and if you over-shoot your objective, great!

The most important thing is to avoid sabotaging yourself with objectives or goals that are far too difficult to reach.

Goal setting will become a discipline that you will learn well in your writing career.

4 - Develop your personal writing system

When do you write best, in the morning or in the evening?

What conditions do you write best under? Background noise, completely quiet, music, etc?

Do you have to be "inspired" to write or can you just sit down and begin writing?

Good writers plan a writing system for their work and do all they can to stick to it.

If the writer is a morning person and functions better before dawn, he may do better work and find more creativity sparking before the family wakes.

Just the same, a sporadic writer may find that he works better under pressure or at odd times of the night or very early mornings. Whichever the mood or the place, a writer must develop a plan and a system for writing whenever the inspiration hits, while analyzing their own personal patterns and when their creativity is at its peak performance.

5- Strategize a marketing plan

Your marketing plan for your writing business is crucial in helping you to decide which way to go with your marketing efforts.

Successful marketing requires a well-thought out, well- outlined and documented effort whether you are home- based or within an office setting.

Develop your marketing plan just as you would any other goal for your copywriting business.

Decide on your goals and target dates for various elements of your marketing plan and implement them, one-by-one.

If you plan to market your writing services to the local chamber of commerce, develop a plan to do this.

You may want to start by attending their monthly luncheons. Then you may want to get involved with some of the other events that they feature during the month.

As you are visiting and networking within these venues, you will distribute your business cards, samples of your work and any other pertinent materials to those potential clients.

All of this may take place over the course of a set period of time as dedicated by your marketing plan.

THE BASIC MECHANISM OF COPYWRITING

Copywriting requires basic mechanics that are conducive to most any type of business. There really aren't any special things to consider in the venue of writing.

However there are certain things that an entrepreneur must focus on in order to make the most of out his copywriting business.

The mechanics of a copywriting business involve using the most basic elements of managing any other home based business.

Home businesses are dependent upon certain principles that keep them viable and strong and on the same level as brick-and-mortar businesses.

These elements are derived from business principles, but are relative to the writing industry as they (the mechanics) are important for the success of the writing business in particular.

1 - Discipline yourself to write

Do you find yourself writing whenever you feel like it and not writing whenever you don't feel like it? This trait can be discouraging and harmful to the copywriter's life and can cause him to lose business.

Any exhibition of this shows a lack of discipline and should be addressed before you embark on the copywriter's lifestyle.

How can you discipline yourself to write?

By writing at a particular, dedicated time each day without fail. Set a schedule for yourself and stick to that schedule no matter what.

The discipline to write can be a challenging one, but once you address it, face it and develop an approach to combat it, discipline will become easier to face and easier to overcome.

2 - Study the elements of other good copy

The best copywriters learn from some of the material written by other copywriter's who are experts in their field.

The aspiring copywriter student will want to glean information and traits from the work of good copywriter's to get an idea of what businesses and clients are looking for in a good writer.

Copy that is well-written will have certain elements that jump out at you as you read and examine it. Ask yourself: Is it visually appealing? Does it look good at first glance? Is there enough white space? Do your eyes work hard to travel the page? Is the text plainly and clearly written? Simple enough but not too simple?

Study magazine and feature articles that show you how well-read and well-presented copy is supposed to look when the reader uses it. Take all available opportunities to study good copywriting when you can.

3 – Read, Read and Read Some More!

All writers are readers. Plain and simple. You cannot write good copy if you aren't willing to read. To be a good copywriter, read everything that is within your niche market...and everything outside of your niche market.

For the aspiring copywriter, reading is going to be more than just reading for the sake of it. You want to read things that are going to spark ideas and thoughts that will help you to develop good copy skills.

In addition to reading outside materials to hone your copywriting skills, take a moment to also read your own materials. When you do read your material, you then have the chance to tweak, adjust and critic your own work.

True, a writer is his own worst critic, but it is far better to critic your own work, being critical, than it is to produce sub-par materials in the name of professional writing.

Read your own copy as well, to improve your level of professionalism and presentation to your clients.

4 - Join writing clubs

What is the purpose of joining and participating in writing clubs? You get the benefit of a critical eye from a jury of your own peers.

Writers always need a "second pair of eyes" to look at their work and critic their material.

Writing clubs can be a huge beneficial resource for writers, both online and offline. Because there are so many genres of writing groups, as a writer, you can become a part of any of them.

The clubs allow you to give and get advice and the opportunity to receive invaluable resources that will enhance your career writing goals.

<Online writing clubs>

Writing clubs that are online can be either a part of forums, communities within websites, specialized blogs or even within chat rooms.

They're easier to find and participate in, but also easier to invite unwanted or unsolicited sales and marketing messages from other participants.

When you are looking for an online writing club, look for clubs or communities that match your specific genre. Try to find those that are specifically customized to your target niche market.

If you are an Internet marketer who specializes in writing on Internet copywriting, find other communities who are concentrated in this area rather than a general audience of online content writers.

Many times, offline writing clubs along with your online resources can help make your writing goals just as attainable as any.

Offline writing clubs can be found at libraries, coffee houses and university lounges and can be just as resourceful as any other.

Do You Have What It Takes To be a Freelance Writer?

More people are finding freelance employment aside from their regular day jobs. They leave the security of their regular employment to move on to the challenges of freelance employment. Freelancing has become a career choice for many who people who enjoy the benefits that it offers. Freelancers often attribute their interest to freelance employment to the following factors:

* Wider range of job opportunities;

* Fast turnaround of projects;

* More freedom to choose projects of choice;

* More flexibility to work on different jobs on a simultaneous basis; and

* High income rates

Do you have what it takes to go freelance? Before you take the plunge and begin the journey of working at home, read through the following steps and tricks.

1. Determine the amount of money that you'll need to earn to sustain your expenses. If you have a day job now, you will be saving a great deal of money once you make your shift to freelance employment. If you begin to work at home, you will save a lot of money from commuting, food, taxes, and more.

2. Take a self-assessment test and list all your skills and experiences. Include your hobbies and interests too, as doing

this will determine what types of freelance jobs you can take on. Do you keep a personal website? Then perhaps you can on freelance web design. Do you keep a personal blog? Then you can take on writing jobs. If you know how to do searches in the internet then you can write about any topic that may be given to you.

3. Visit internet web sites offering freelance jobs to see what jobs are currently offered. Take notes and keep a list of these jobs. You should also be on the lookout for companies and organizations that use freelancers for their projects. Look at how much they pay freelancers and take note of the different rates they offer for different projects. Keep a list of these important details as they will surely help you later in estimating how much you should charge for any given project.

4. From the notes you have gathered, try to create an estimate costing of the projects you have identified should the projects be given to you. Keep in mind the number of days given to the projects you have identified. When you have done this, you will be able to see how much you could potentially earn.

5. After doing all of the above, you can now start applying for the freelance jobs that you have identified. These jobs will help you earn some amount that you can later use after quitting you day job.

6. Once you have confirmed that the projects have been awarded to you, use a table to plot specific data about them. Write down all the information about these projects such as contact persons and their contact details and number of days to complete the projects.

7. As you begin freelance work, you will start to feel the flow of freelance employment. Bear in mind that you will not get all the projects that you want so you should apply for different jobs. However, be careful when taking on several jobs. Remember that you should not take on more jobs than you could handle.

8. You are now ready to quit your day job when you have developed an effective system of doing freelance work. But since you are doing freelance work, you should be able to track your jobs and their payment schedules.

What qualifications do you need in your home business to become an effective copywriter?

The Qualifications for a Freelance writer

The home business writer often has to market and strategize his efforts differently and more creative than his counterparts who are in the corporate sector.

Because he doesn't always have the benefit of a staff or other contractors, the home business writer has to be effectively creative jut to stay competitive.

The home business writer has to hone his skills and keep himself above the learning and technology curve in order to stand out from the crowd.

Clients want to hire writers with skills that convert lookers into buyers. They want excellent copy written for their products or services. If they hire you, you need to be able to provide them with these skills.

What qualifications do you need in your home business to become an effective copywriter?

1 - The ability to create compelling copy

If you cannot write gripping text with persuadable words, you will have difficulty making successful ventures and satisfying your clients. Compelling words full of action and energy is what moves buyers to buy.

Practice writing compelling copy, by writing compelling copy. Use action words in your daily communications (wherever possible) and always make sure the copy is something that will make you move as well.

Keep your copy freshly compelling by studying buzz words and action phrases that get consumers to want to buy. Words and phrases like:

- For a limited time
- Act Now
- Buy Now
- You will experience..
- Your life will change..
- Exclusive Offer

And substitute inactive words and phrases for their opposite. For instance:

Instead of "if you would like more information on..." Say, "email us at xxx@abc.com for more information." Instead of "for a copy"…

Say, "Get your copy today while they last" Instead of saying, "…if you need XX product"…,

Say, " this product will do XXX for you. Order here".

The difference in your choice of words and how you order and align the words can mean a world of difference in your copy and how well that copy will convert.

2 - The ability to persuade an audience

Do you have the ability to persuade readers to do what you want them to do? Very few people have the skill and charisma to persuade persons, interested or not, into doing something that they otherwise would not do.

Persuading an audience towards your interests is a skill that can be learned. Studying and learning the habits of people can help you to write compelling copy to get them to buy. What are some things you can do to help you study your audience and win them over?

a.) Identify with your audience

Share with them things that are commonly found in your niche audience. Find a commonality and expound on it while you are writing your copy.

Don't embellish, as it really is not necessary. But rather, find something that the audience can nod to and see themselves in your text.

For instance, if you are writing a copy piece on selling personal security products, you want to find a common thread among your readers.

b.) Be honest

Always tell your audience the truth. Be honest and open and tell them not what they want to hear about your product or service, but what actually the truth about it is.

Being honest in your writing helps to connect to the audience by giving them insight into your context of writing. They are more apt to believe plausible, sensible claims than outrageous claims.

Although it's alright to be motivational and inspirational, moving the audience to action, but be careful to not embellish the text and promise things that cannot be delivered.

3 - The ability to sell and/or market your skills

Are you able to market your writing well? Can you find resources where you can showcase your writing talents and abilities to find clients?

If you are able to market and sell well, you should be able to find it relatively easy to market your writing abilities too.

Be smart and creative with your writing resources and places where you can market them. Don't feel like you have to "sell" potential clients. But, you can market your services by sharing essential information and asking the client for the sale.

4 - The ability to seize opportunities as they become available.

Opportunities for writing projects abound all over for copywriters. The need for writing services exists in most all industries so that there should never really be a shortage of jobs at any time.

The opportunity to write can be created as well by asking for more opportunity from existing clients or by asking for referrals from friends and acquaintances that are also in the writing industry.

If you have begun establishing writing clients for your business, ask them for either repeat business or referrals as you complete each project. If you do a great job, deliver as promised and produce quality work, getting more work should not be a problem at all for you.

You can also create opportunities by volunteering your services to non-profit or good cause organizations.

These establishments are always in need of good, well-written copy material and could use your help.

Create the opportunity by asking for referrals from the non-profit client after you have completed a project for them.

JOHN ROBERTSON

Becoming Invaluable By Making Your Client's Life Easier

The best clients are the busy clients. Why? Because they're the ones with successful businesses, so they have enough money to pay you. They're also the ones who are busy enough that they really need you. And they're the ones who are likely to have ongoing work for you.

They're also the ones who are the easiest to keep because you know exactly what you need to do to keep them. It's simple – just make their life easier and save them as much time as possible and they'll come back.

It may seem like a simple thing, but it will make a big difference to clients. I know because I've spoken to hundreds of clients and have constantly been told how busy they are.

Making it Easy for Clients

Making a client's life easy is simple to do. All you have to do is remember that the client is busy every time you contact them and think about how you can make it easier for them. Here's a good example for a freelancer who was asked to send a brief overview stating the angle and content of the article.

First Example of Brief to Client

After a lot of thought and research, I have decided that the angle of the article will focus on effective ways of trading shares on a budget. I plan to cover three main topics. These will be new floats, low-cost shares, and how to reduce trading costs.

Second Example of Brief to Client

Angle: Trading Shares on a Budget

Content:

- New floats

- Low-cost shares

- Reducing trading costs

Both examples communicate the same meaning. But the example with headings and bullets is much easier to read. The busy client can learn exactly what they need to know with little more than a glance. It also has a more professional and organized look and so creates a better impression of you.

And as a final added bonus, the easiest way for the client is also the easiest and quickest way for you. So, you win a little extra time and quite possibly a long-term client.

A Final Tip

Remember that if clients seem rushed, they probably are. If clients seem stressed, they probably are. Don't think of it as a bad thing – think of it as a great opportunity.

If you can be one of the people that makes life easier and takes away some of the stress, you've got yourself a client that is likely to pay you well and pay you often. And that's what a successful freelancer needs to succeed.

JOHN ROBERTSON

JUMPING INTO FREELANCE COPYWRITING

With the advent of technology, copywriting already covers a wide range of media like television, radio, magazines, brochures, direct mail, and the like today. In fact, every word in every brochure, advert, website and leaflet you see is written by the copywriter. Before, copywriters are restricted to being in-house or by marketing / PR firms but now, there are so many freelance copywriters that offer their services.

But, doing a freelance copywriting job can be quite stressful. Just like all freelance jobs, freelance copywriting means that you have to sell or market yourself, your ability to meet a deadline or complete a job on time, and to budget resources by making use of your skills and knowledge.

Being a copywriter enables you to choose a specific or particular market sector or product and you are expected to write something or anything that your potential client wishes. In order to become a good and successful copywriter, you should have a great ability to research about a certain topic while understanding your clients and target customers.

Aside from having excellent research and understanding skills, you also have to have imagination and flair to keep you ideas running while keeping your clients happy.

Being A Copywriter

Just like the existence of so many different copies to be written, there are also different types of copywriters in the market today. Some of which are those who have specialization in very specific forms of copywriting like direct mail or ad copy while there are those who take a more general approach by writing copies for any item that is available.

Today, freelance copywriters are known to write different forms of copy and are expected to produce great outputs. But, despite being demanding work, freelance copywriting can be a lot of fun and one of the best ways make great money if you have the skill, the connection, and the drive to be successful.

Aside from being an avenue to earn great income, freelance copywriting also offers you the ability to work from anywhere via Internet. If you are planning to become a freelance copywriter, then here are some tips that can help you do the job:

1. Get educated. If you want to delve into the world of freelance copywriting, then it is a must that you get any type of writing degree in English, Journalism, Communications, and the like. Having an education or a background on the career you wish to pursue can be a strong step in finding work as a copywriter.

If is it's impossible for you to have a degree, try to get certifications or non-degree courses that teach copywriting basics offered by many colleges. Having a background on copywriting can serve as your credential once you venture into freelance work.

2. Get a pro bono work. If you don't have any other experience, writing a copy or an item for free will provide you the experience you need. The copies you have written can also serve as sample copies once you market yourself as a freelance copywriter.

3. Try to get an internship. An internship from an establishment known to the field you wish to pursue can definitely back up your credentials once your venture as a freelance copywriter. Aside from giving you experience and

first-hand knowledge, an internship may also lead you to a permanent employment with the company.

4. Consider various opportunities. Since the industry is booming, there are lots of freelance copywriters out there who serve as your competitors. If you are really into freelance copywriting, then you should always be updated with businesses and agencies that may need copywriting services. Make sure that you check local newspapers regularly.

Freelamce Writing : The Essentials

In the industry of freelancing, among the most in demand are writers. This is especially true with the birth of the Internet, which tripled the need for writers because of the various websites and online content that are constantly being updated.

There are actually lots of work that a freelance writer can go into especially if they have established the right contacts. Freelance writers, as mentioned, are needed for writing online content to boost website viewership. In fact, online content is fast becoming one of the major sources of freelance assignments not only for writers but also for other freelancers such as photographers, web designers and graphic artists.

But though there are lots of assignments and freelance jobs waiting on the sidelines, this does not mean that you'll be getting a fair share of them. Because just as there are lots of jobs, there are also lots of freelance writers that you have to compete with. To make sure that you stay competitive, here are some tips.

Self-market

If you plan to do freelancing, make sure that people know that you do freelance. How else will they know unless you tell them? It's not as if you can advertise and that is an added cost that most people cannot afford. When you meet people, don't hesitate to give them your card and to tell them that you do freelance work. Self-marketing is essential as this will give you the contacts that you need in order to start a freelance career. This is especially true with people who are working in similar industry like writers for magazines, webzines and other publications.

Always Try do your best

Because you are actually doing the work that you are doing in the company that you work for, it is important that you always do your best and to make sure that you take care of your work reputation. Your work, whether they are PR write-ups or newspaper articles, will be the basis for you being commissioned for freelance work. So make sure that you always give your best in every assignment.

Establish a sound and solid reputation

It is not only your work that you should take care of but also your attitude in dealing with people. You can be the most brilliant writer but if you are known in the industry as difficult to work with, you will find it hard to get side lines and freelance jobs. Take care of your reputation especially in terms of work ethics and meeting deadlines as these are important factors that employers consider in hiring freelance writers.

Look for jobs

Of course, it is not also right that you just wait for people to give you work. You can actually look for assignments yourself, just to tide you over before actual assignments come in. There are many ways to look for freelancing jobs.

You can log on to job sites where they have a special section that features freelancing jobs or part time jobs. Some are even located in different states, which you can actually accept since most just require telecommuting and not your actual presence.

Another way to look for jobs is to ask people that you know for referrals. This way, you can use the contacts that you have established in your profession.

Home Business Set-Up

As you are setting up your home business, be very careful to consider all elements of your personality and work style when you are choosing the layout, design and plan of your writing style.

Setting it up the RIGHT way

When it comes time to set up a copywriting business, many entrepreneurs skimp on some areas and give attention to other, less important areas. This is not good as it can cause imbalance in how things are managed and what issues get top priorities.

Your copywriting business is your livelihood and should be treated just as confidently as a brick-and-mortar business would. Establishing your copywriting business as a viable source within a competitive market will be the best thing that you can do for it.

There are some must-do's within the writing market that can enhance your writing career and help you satisfy your niche market.

The ten "I's"

As you are writing and progressing towards your goal of becoming a seasoned copywriter online, there are investments that you must make in your business that will pay off in the long run.

1 - Invest in a desktop

Investing in a good, reliable and hearty computer that can withstand the rigors of the constant writing lifestyle. This is not an area to skimp since this is the lifeblood of your home business.

I suggest you also purchase a cloud service or backup software. This includes spam ware or malware and software programs for your system's backup.

Backing up your system often is necessary as well. This will be critical for those times if and when (hopefully never) you ever experience a systems failure and possibly lose everything. Your desktop computer should be well-equipped to handle any conceivable situation.

2 - Invest in a good laptop

As it relates to flexibility and convenience, this is likely one of the main accessories that you will use in your writing career.

Portable and accessible, a laptop is the idea accompaniment for you if you are very busy with your writing and if you are rarely able to actually work from your desktop.

3 - Invest in a good printer

Printers come in many forms and types, so find one that's suitable for you. There really is no need to over-buy in this area as much of a copywriter's work is done via online and in digital format.

If you are an offline-based copywriter, it would be highly advantageous for you to invest in a good printer that will make your final copy look brilliant.

Look for copiers that have a high resolution output with basic print options. Once you print a copy for proofing, you will likely send this to your client in digital format for editing.

4 - Invest in a fax machine

Fax machines aren't a LARGE staple for the online copywriter but are necessary nonetheless. However, a basic fax should be sufficient.

You are likely to use the fax machine for basic communications and for sending and receiving bids and quotes that need signatures. It's important to be as professional as possible with your clients.

5 - Invest in business cards

Business cards are a business staple that will never go out of style. They are necessary for every phase of your business and can help to increase your business even more.

Make your business cards very basic for a professional, no frills look. Save the glitz and the glamour for the

graphic image designers. In copywriting, your words are your proof. Make them all count.

6 - Invest in quality furniture

The main item in a writer's lifestyle as it relates to furniture is his chair. Without the right chair, the writer will not be able to fully focus or be comfortable, and that can result in poor work production.

Invest in a chair that does not make you slouch or crouch down in the chair. Make sure the back is high and straight with a slight profusion for the lower back.

Other office amenities are not so important for the entrepreneur starting out. However, another important item next to the correct type of chair is the level of the desktop or laptop that he will be using to produce his work on.

If the level of the desktop doesn't comfortably meet your eye, you could experience eye strain and fatigue. Investing early in this type of equipment is sure to be well worth its weight in value!

7 - Invest in quality lighting

Writing for long and lengthy periods of time can become fatiguing. Improper lighting can cause even more of a physical distress as you try to work.

Get quality lighting for your business office and increase your productivity. If it's difficult for you to see your copy as you work, you are likely to make mistakes and errors that are sometimes irreversible.

8 - Invest in a library of reference books

You should always keep an arsenal of good copywriting books within your library as reference for your copywriting business. Refer to these books for tips, information, guidelines and general support for your target niche area. Some good books to stock your library with can include:

9 - Invest in people

People are what help your business and what you need to keep it afloat. Investing in people is simply being available as a business source, a point of reference or to act as a problem solver. When you invest in people, they will remember it and reciprocate as appropriate.

10 - Invest in your goals

Take the time to realize your goals and the investment that you have in them.

 - Are you investing time in realizing the fruition of your goals?

 - Are you investing the quality into them to ensure their success?

These are crucial points to your goals and making them all work for you.

How are copywriters inspired?

What inspires you as a copywriter and makes you want to learn more about your craft? There are many areas of inspiration that a copywriter can use to spark his creativity and find topics.

1 - Through reading

Read work and materials written by others. This will spark new ideas, slants on old ideas and provide you with thought-inspired material for your own business.

2 - Through participating

The best way to learn something is to do it. Many writers jump start their careers by participating in writing contests, submitting short articles or fiction articles to magazines, or by working through other venues where they can release their creativity.

3 - Momentary inspiration

Many writers can be inspired by what is happening at the moment. They look around them for inspiration and ideas in their everyday lives. They then take these simple things and transfer them over into their targeted niche areas and glean inspiration.

4 - As a problem solver

Give a copywriter a problem...and he'll likely solve it! That should be the goal of every copywriter's vision. Solving their problems in terms of good copy and well- structured content will make the copywriter an online hero of sorts.

How To Get Lucrative Freelance Writing Jobs

No matter where you live, landing lucrative writing assignments does not need to be difficult. The secret to a profitable freelance writing career is to start small and build it from there. Another secret... you must remember to promote your business on a REGULAR basis. Do not shoot off a few ads or letters, then wait three months before launch another campaign. Promote your business DAILY.

Here are some of the BEST Techniques to get work:

Technique #1: Approach your local newspaper editor.

Ask if they need a freelancer to cover city council, school board, and/or county board meetings. If they do, you are on your way earning a living as a writer because you are about to earn tons of clips. You will also start making valuable business contacts. More on that later...

Technique #2: Expand To Bigger Markets

Armed with your local clips, you can start approaching bigger freelance markets. Markets like small and mid-sized magazines that are hungry for new articles. Start querying them and wait for their response.

Technique #3: Don't be afraid to approach work

While you are waiting to hear from your magazine queries, chat with few of the mayors, city council people, school board members, etc. that you have met at your meetings. Most of them are business people. Ask if they need a freelancer to update their brochures, write ads or direct mail letters, or if they need a writer-for-hire for a project they have brewing. You would be surprised how many business people will take you up on your offer after they have witnessed your diligence and accuracy while covering their meetings.

Technique #4: Go Local!

Now target local businesses and contact them. Offer to write their marketing materials.

Technique #5: Ads do wonders sometimes...

To start attracting more commercial clients, run a small ad in your local paper. As your expertise increases, place more ads in surrounding papers.

Technique #6: Expand To Bigger Markets

Join your local Chamber of Commerce. You will meet even more business owners who may need a freelance writer and you will make invaluable contacts.

Technique #7: Direct Mail and/or Newsletter

Send out a direct mail piece advertising your writing services. If you are not comfortable writing direct mail, you can put together a newsletter. Target the businesses you would like to work with and make sure you contact them on a regular basis.

Another technique to keep the money rolling in as a freelance writer is to keep lots of irons in the fire. Along with the magazine queries and copywriting, always have a book in the works and send publishers proposals for it.

Technique #8: Take on Special Projects

Another idea: I know one local freelancer who has cultivated a devoted clientele who has her write all their correspondence... including Christmas letters. Your projects are limited only by your imagination.

Technique #9: Goal Setting Ritual

Make goals each day. Decide how many queries you will send out. Decide how many sales letters you will mail. How many words are you going to write in your book? How many new contacts are you going to make this week? Make your goals... then follow through with them.

Technique #10: Referrals

Ask and you may receive. Do not be afraid to ask for what you want. If you are a stringer for your local newspaper, ask the editor if it is possible for them to run a small ad promoting your business at a discount (after all you are a staff writer.) If you write for local businesses, ask them to recommend your writing services to their friends.

Technique #11: Be Assertive

Never tell anyone your phone number. GIVE it to them. Print a bunch of business cards and whenever anyone asks for your phone number, give them your card instead.

Technique #12: The Importance of Networking

Network. Make friends in the freelance writing. Give each other leads and help each other become the best writers you can be.

Technique #13: Have a Portfolio at hand

Carry your latest project with you. If you have written a book, bring it wherever you go. If you just finished a big copywriting project, have it nearby. Got an article in the latest issue of a magazine or newspaper? Better bring it with you.... Nothing sparks a conversation faster than "What 'cha been up to lately?" Then, next thing you know, you have got a prospective customer.

I know, I know... I promised twelve strategies to start making money ASAP as a freelance writer. But I got on a roll and thirteen (I have heard) is an unlucky number so here is one more strategy.

Read. Read everything you can get your hands on. If you write novels, read novels. If you write direct mail, read EVERY piece of direct mail that land on your doorstep. If you write ads, read ads. Read what your competition is writing. Read what your friends are writing. Make note of what "works" for you and what does not. Then write something better.

Read e-mags that will help you make your writing as sharp as possible. Perfect your craft, become the best writer you can be, promote your business, and you will have more work than you can handle.

So there you have it. Fourteen fantastic strategies to land lucrative writing assignments and make a great living as a freelance writer. The possibilities are endless. Find out what works for you, then run with it. You just may find yourself earning a very nice income.

Where to Look for Freelance Copywriting Jobs

You can find that there are numerous freelance copywriting jobs out there. Within this article today, we'll look at a couple of the different websites and how you can make sure to set yourself apart from all of the other freelancers out there.

Our first task is to identify the different marketplaces where you should have a subscription. The website that will be profiled first is www.elance.com. This particular marketplace has a very strong following as more than 100,000 potential customers come by the website each week. You are able to sign up to sell your services and the system allows you to upload your best work to sell yourself to potential clients. There is also a search agents in place so that you can have jobs that meet your criteria e-mailed to you on a daily basis. Cost for a subscription to this particular website can range from eight dollars per month up to one hundred twenty dollars per month.

The second website which you should look to register for it is www.guru.com. This is actually the largest online freelance marketplace on the Internet to look for online jobs including freelance copywriting jobs. The capabilities of this website are similar to the ones that were posted in the paragraph above for that particular website. It has a service provider base of over 481,000 people. If you live in Europe, you can use both of these websites as well as a European challenge to these two, which is found at www.getafreelancer.com. There are many other websites that also offer a freelance online marketplace and one of these is www.directfreelance.com.

This should get you started in being able to find different websites and which you can bid on projects. When you are bidding on projects, companies that are looking at the bids will not be looking just at price but also at how their work will be done. To do this you will want to set yourself apart.

The way that you can set yourself apart in creating a bid is to include copies of your best work but also make sure that you include testimonials along with a sales letter on why you will be the best party bidding on this particular project. By doing this, you will be tailoring your message to the particular party and you will be showing them examples of your past work along with happy clients. This will help improve your credibility and firmly anchor you as a potential candidate who can get the job done.

Many copywriters do not have a website today so if you take the opportunity to create a website, you will find that you could have a competitive advantage in the freelance copywriting jobs market.

It is important to know which websites you should use in finding work but it is also important to find ways to set yourself apart. By creating a website as well as creating an advertising package that shows off your best side, you are setting yourself up to stand apart from other freelancers. You are selling yourself when you create this package so keep that in mind.

Where You Can Find Freelance Writing Opportunities

Freelancing work is one of the major sources of extra income nowadays. The profession has been so lucrative that people leave their work sometimes in order to do freelance full time.

This is of course not recommended for people who are not yet established in the industry. In order to do full time freelance, you have to make sure that you have the contacts to back you up and the extra money to tide you over when freelance work is not so many. Remember that freelancing is not a stable profession.

Unlike with working for a regular company, freelancing does guarantee a steady income. Assignments come in trickles. Some months will find you with many assignment while others months will give you none. This is why it is also important to know how to budget your money and to have savings that you can use in case of unforeseen expenses.

When you think about it, it is not really hard to look for freelance writing opportunities. In fact, a lot of writing jobs especially freelance, have opened up because of the increasing demand for people who can update online content. In addition to the other areas and industries that they can write in, websites have given them greater number of potential assignments and jobs.

Still, where you will write or what kind of freelance writing you will do will depend entirely on what know and where your expertise lies. This is actually one of the great things about freelancing. You get to do the things that you already know how to do. In addition to earning more money, you are also gaining experience and enriching yourself through training.

Below are some of the areas and industries where freelance writers are needed. Read on and find the freelance path that is right for you.

Magazines

Freelance writers are frequently hired to contribute articles for magazines. In fact, this is one area where you can actually get regular assignments as freelance writer especially if they find your work good. The rate for every article is quite generous especially if it involves interview. Some writers even kill two birds with one stone by also taking the photographs for the interview. This way, they are also paid for the pictures that are published.

Newspaper correspondent

Another area where you can get freelance work are the newspapers, who often hire correspondents. This is especially true with areas that are outside the city. Newspapers find it cheaper to hire correspondents and pay for their services than send their own writers to coverages and provide for their transportation.

Online writers

As mentioned before, online writers are in demand nowadays because writers are needed to update the online content in websites. The writing industry online is so on the upswing that magazines that keep their own websites hire writers just to do online content. In fact, not all the write ups that you see in the Internet can be found in the magazines and not all articles in the magazines are used for online content.

PR writing

Public relations writing is the new and more effective way to advertise products. Because of this, companies are often hiring writers to do their pr write ups for them. This is because not only one article should be done. One topic or even is rehashed in several ways to fit different sections in publications.

JOHN ROBERTSON

TIPS IN GETTING FREELANCE WRITING

One of the best things about being a writer is the fact that you can hold a permanent job and still write on the side. That is the good thing in having a creative profession. You can do sidelines and freelancing jobs while still being salaried regularly. In fact, many writers in magazines and newspapers accept writing and editing jobs on the side while others who can afford not to have a permanent job will settle in with freelance jobs.

Actually, there are some freelancing jobs that can pay a lot and can even exceed a person's monthly pay. Permanent writing jobs however provide the security. You wouldn't want to wake up one morning without money to pay for the rent, right?

Freelance writing jobs are a dime a dozen especially with the advent of Internet. Writers are frequently commissioned to do online content to keep websites updated and informative. Still, one needs to know where to look and how to look if you want to get regular assignments. Below are some tips in getting freelance writing jobs

Go online.

There are a number of writing jobs that one can find in the internet and what is more, these freelance jobs can be accomplished at home. Some do not even require you to pass the articles in person. Because of the great convenience that the internet provides, telecommuting is already possible.

This means that you don't have to physically go to work. You can just submit your works online. Payments for these kinds of jobs are often deposited through bank transfers.

You can find freelance work listings in websites that feature freelance works. Some jobsites also have listings of these kinds of assignments.

Establish a network

Being a writer, you have to establish a network of people who will later on recommend you for jobs and writing assignments. PR professionals for instance look for writers who can do assignments for them. The same goes with owners of companies that advertise over the internet or those who maintain websites which you can write for. Editors of magazines and newspapers are also often in the lookout for writers in publications.

There are a lot of people who are looking for part-time or freelance writers and the bigger your network is, the more people you can associate with who can help you.

Ask for a referral or a recommendation

The first step in asking for a referral is to do a damn good job that people will want to refer you to another. Although writing is big business, the industry is actually pretty small. Chances are your boss in one project will also know someone who is doing a similar project. Ask for a recommendation to another person who is in need of a writer or better yet ask them if they know someone who might be looking for a freelance writer. This is one way to get assignments.

Write Well

The key to having a great freelancing career is to take care of your reputation not only in terms of your writing but also in the way you deal with people. For instance, you can write so well but if you are always late in passing your assignments, no person would want to deal with you. Remember that writing involves deadlines and you have to keep up with it if you want to really stay in the industry.

MARKETING YOUR SERVICES

Ok, let's go over the best practices to marketing your freelance writing work. This is a crucial part, as you probably can already tell that you need clients to market your work to. So in this chapter, we'll discuss the marketing process,

1 - Giving samples of your work

Giving out samples of your work as a copywriter shows your potential clients what you're capable of doing. It gives them a good idea of your writing style and ability. Samples can show how well you can write on tightly focused topics and stay within the subject.

Samples by the very definition will be free to the potential client. Samples are only meant to be a "sampler" and should not include previously written work for other clients.

To avoid having your samples of writing stolen, save your file as a PDF before forwarding it to the client. This presents professionally and also helps you to avoid any particularly embarrassing situations with your intellectual property being misused.

Samples will help you in marketing in several different ways:

(1) The potential client may refer you to others based on your sampling work alone.

(2) Always attach a by-line to the end of your work, including samples, and it will always accompany your intellectual property.

(3) You can use samples of your work at trade shows or as a stand alone piece in your marketing kit.

Don't think of sampling as giving something away more so than receiving potential business. Your samples give your target audience a peek into what you can produce as a copywriter.

2 - Use free resources/advertising

Advertising resources that are free are a gold mine for a copywriter! Knowing where and when to look for those resources can become a marketing heaven for the writer. Here he can use his hard skills as a writer to craft compelling copy for his advertising pitch.

Copywriting alone is a free resource for advertising for the writing services that he has. Whatever type of writing that the home business entrepreneur is in helps steer him towards the right direction for finding free resources.

Businesses that are related to the type of business that you operate are ideal for advertising in. You can "stack" your advertising against the competition when you approach the source.

Stacking is when two or more businesses are advertising the same product or service. It's very common of course in certain niches, but can be beneficial for all interested parties.

Target those businesses and free resources that have a theme. Do this by focusing on the theme and personality of the publication that you're targeting.

A theme will be better for the product in the long run than if you just have random ideas that are thrown together.

If you are a copywriter focusing on children's products, a newsletter publication about parenting is far likely to review your writing abilities and pitches than a car magazine would be.

Stay on themes (if possible) and stay focused.

Approach any local businesses and ask them to place ads in their free newsletters or sales circular letters that are distributed to the public.

In exchange for this advertising, offer them a copywriting project either at a discount or bartered for exchange. This works well for small businesses that can exchange goods and services fairly easily.

Some classified advertising in many local newspapers is free, depending upon what is offered and how much value is in the service.

There are also online bulletin boards that will allow you to advertise or market your services, provided that there is no over-saturation of your marketing message and no blatant spamming.

Many free resources often ask for donations or have a limit or cap on how much of your free message they will advertise within a given time period. To avoid this, cycle how many times and when you will approach a free resource about advertising.

This rotation will keep your approach and message fresh, and keep readers from feeling "sold" or "spammed" every time they see your message.

Simple Methods Of Marketing Your Copywriting Business

There are many creative ways and ideas that you can use to market your copywriting business, both online and offline to your customers.

These ideas are simply guides and tools that you can loosely use in order to jumpstart your career path or add to the services that you already offer.

1 - Write

The first and foremost marketing idea that you can use in pursuit of more business is to do what you do best as a writer, and that is to write.

Write about your niche market and distribute it as a free report or as an add-on to the other services that you offer. Focus on and highlight the strengths of copywriting and how they can enhance your customer's bottom line. Keep the focus on the benefits that the customer will receive.

2 - Join social circles

The Internet has become the ideal place for businesses and individuals to connect. They find more business and referrals abound for those who are specialists in their area(s) of expertise. How do people find out about them? Through social media sites and forums.

There are many social sites where you can establish an online presence and find new business. Most of the popular ones include:

- -Facebook
- -Twitter
- -LinkedIn

These are not all encompassing but do share the bulk of the online audiences that refer to them for professional services.

Create a profile on these and any other networks that you can find and market them just as you would any other tool.

3 - Hold seminars

Using your local community, you can hold seminars and workshops on copywriting and resources for the lifestyle. This will give you a chance to share your information with the general public AND get your name in front of the community.

Seminars and workshop-type environments bring out people who are curious and interested in getting more information about a particular topic. If there are any decision-makers in your audience, you have just created an opportunity for your services.

4 - Use media sources

This means free advertising that's given by television, radio and the news stations, if appropriate. Ask and seek out resources from the media's perspective that will bring your copywriting business more exposure for your services.

Media sources can also include blogs, news websites, chat rooms, custom forums that are online.

Offline sources may include clubs, networks or chapters that are focused on your genre of writing and copy style. Determine which one is best for you and which works better for your industry.

5 - Use press releases

Press releases are ideal for marketing your services and giving information on new and improved features of your business services.

Release press releases often enough to be interesting but not too often as to saturate the market and bore your audience.

6 - Custom letters

Custom letters are usually written directly to a person or an organization with an express purpose in mind.

These custom letters will address the fact that you are a writer and you're introducing yourself as such.

Write letter directly to magazine editors, introduce yourself and let them know that you wish to establish a business relationship. You will likely gain a lot of business from them because of your creative approach.

Even if they don't gain any new business, the lasting impression that you create will be well worth it.

7 - Referrals/Testimonials

The best thing that anyone could ever do when they're happy is to tell someone else. As a copywriter, you hope that it happens everyday.

Happy customers tell other happy (potential) customers and hopefully the cycle continues. If as a copywriter you deliver quality services, your work will begin to speak for itself and the work will start flowing in.

8 - Self-publishing

As a self-publisher for your own materials, you can self publish your own books and make them available to your potential market. Let your work speak for itself.

9 - Blitzes

Do marketing blitzes with friends and peers in the same niche category. These blitzes help each of you find your core areas of strengths and pluses to approach clients.

10 - Use direct mail

Promote your services using direct mail services. Send this information to business within your target area and industry.

11 - Classifieds

Classified advertising is the best venue to advertise your services as a copywriter. It is a free resource and found to be lucrative both online and offline.

12 - Non-profits

Writing for the non-profit sector can be a good source of marketing for your copywriting business and also good for the non-profit's business.

13 - Your signature

Use the Internet to promote yourself through e-mail signatures, articles, Web sites and links and live conferences.

Elements of Effective Sales Copy: The Sales Page

Effective sales copy elicits response from the reader and gets him to make a decision based on what he has read.

The sales copy is divided up into three sections:

1 - Headline

The headline is the attention-grabbing portion of the text. This is where you will catch the reader's eye and make him want to read more of the material. You only have a short window of opportunity here to connect with your reader so it's important to make it compelling. Your headline should be relatively short, catchy and inspiring. Try to make your title as lasting as you can, and if you cn put some creativity into it – all the better!

2 - Body

The body is the crux of the copy written material. This is where you will provide your succinct, detailed information and elaborate on the headline of your sales page. The body of the text will discuss and answer questions that the reader may have and enlighten him on more about the product or service.

3 – Conclusion

The body of the sales page will need to be as detailed and well-researched as possible without being too lengthy as to lose the reader. Keep the copy on focus by discussing and detailing the topic in depth.

Copywriting very basically and simply entices your audience to buy your product or service.

In order for you to provide well-written copy to entice them to buy, there are distinctive elements to a sales copy page that engage the reader, encouraging him to read more about your offer is. The principles are based on the AIDA (Attention, Interest, Desire, Action) concept and can be adapted to any copywriting experience.

Attention and Interest

The interest would include the title, the headline and the attention-grabbing portion of the sales copy. The headline should be written in a way that almost yells at your reader. Make it stand out and command attention. Make it noticeable. Examples of headlines include:

Good: How to Start a Lucrative Internet Business

Better: 5 Days to a Profitable Online Business

Best: Automated Success in 10 Easy Steps!

The first headline would get most reader's attention, but if you use the third headline, you are far more likely to get them and keep them reading through your copy to the end.

Your copy's goal here is to catch your reader's attention and create interest. Your topic or point of interest must be compelling enough to bring him in, keep him there and create a desire for more.

Desire

The reader is interested, and now wants what you're offering. The next piece of your focused copy page is to spark and stoke the embers that the interested reader has.

Here, you have the reader's attention. You should write copy that will make them want more. For example:

Do you want to shed those last ten pounds? Of course you do! This revolutionary new product has been on the market for a short period of time, but has caused sensational results with users. With this product, you can get ready for the beach scene in less than 30 days and look great!

After reading this (or similar text), the reader should want more of your offerings and will continue until he reaches the goal of the sales page.

That goal is the entire precept that the marketing page is structured behind. The sales page ends with a call to action, an order form for your clients.

Action

The call to action should be the most concentrated effort of your sales copy. Write towards the reader as if they've already decided that they do want the product or service. Write as if you're thinking in past terms:

Don't ask:

Are you convinced yet that you need this XXX product? Is there anything more that we can say to you to convince you? If so, contact us at xxx-xxxx today!

Say:

This product has the ability to enhance your life giving you more time and freedom to do the things you enjoy. Click here to order now and we'll include an additional 30-day supply of this product just for placing your order on xx/xx/xxxx!

Bonus Chapter: Freelance Paralegal (Advanced)

Like any other profession, individuals who have already experienced working in a law firm for a couple of years begin to be a freelance paralegal for a variety of reasons. A lot of them say that they get the advantage of having a flexible schedule because they owe their time and they do not have an immediate boss who will lord it over them. In other words, their very selves are their direct supervisors.

A freelance paralegal as defined by the National Federation of Paralegal Association (NFPA) is just the same with a traditional legal assistant who is retained on an as- needed basis by their director be it a lawyer or manager, depending on the nature of work. He or she should have undergone formal schooling and have been trained to execute loads of in the field of law.

You may have heard of an independent paralegal who is referred to as a forms practitioner or document preparer. There is actually a huge disparity between them and a freelance paralegal. This is because they continue their tasks sans an attorney overseeing them. Most of the time, it is not considered as legally substantive but clerical in scope. It is also delivered immediately to the customer or client.

In the new millennium, freelance paralegal work has taken shape in many successful grounds be it in the corporate jungle, business world or legal arena. It does not mean that when you are tied up in the study of judicial process in your college years, you will exclusively end up in such. There are actually plenty of other avenues such as:

Developed companies who feature performing an administrative work and at the same moment, train employees for them to have an actual practice themselves.

Partnership dealing who offer diversity of services such as legal typing, court assistance and many others. It would be best if they are accredited with the National Association of Legal Assistants (NALA), if they are based in the United States, for a board verification of their career.

Disparate environments like becoming a software salesperson, computer instructor or academic professor can be your job description. Another is that you will be assigned in a placement firm where you will screen those who would apply.

However, it is not just as simple as what you think it is for it is also coupled with several responsibilities to the paralegal profession, to the lawyers as your boss and to the lawyer's clients who you will also be closely working with. You are also required to comply with taxation laws, federal regulations and commerce laws. What usually happens is that the time you spend in your work is also the same as that of a legitimate attorney.

Conclusion

I really hope you start taking action right now and go for your first freelance writing gig. I want to emphasize that taking action, in any field of work, is key. Reading is one thing, buy if you don't go and implement what you learned – you won't ever be able to start your online career or substitute your current one.

However, if you take into account the fact that today there are more oppurtunities to work online than ever before – you'll be well on your way.

Final Words

In conclusion, if you want to be a successful copywriter on the Internet, you must learn how to write convincingly. This is the only way to build your business and be successful. Anything less would be a disservice to your business.

Begin with a good product or service and go from there. Make sure there is a large interested group of people, and write compelling text towards that market. Tweak the text until it converts lookers and your conversion rate for your clients is high and climbing.

Once your copywriting techniques meet these criteria, then you can get enhance and promote your writing benefits and results. Provide solutions to remedies or answer questions to problems. Either one offer potential customers a reason to do business with you.

By providing solutions problems, you can sell by convincing the person who reads your work that it will be the solution they're seeking. That's why you must start off telling them about the main benefit of problem solving that you are offering.

When you are writing, become your customer. Think like he thinks. Feel what he feels. Know the solution to his problem.

Solutions are what make customers come back for more. When they do, they will find you and continue pushing your career to new heights as a copywriter in high demand.

To your success,

--- John Robertson

www.ingramcontent.com/pod-product-compliance
Lightning Source LLC
Chambersburg PA
CBHW060410190526
45169CB00002B/836